D0429194

The Appletree Book
of
Celtic Verse

First published in 1999
by The Appletree Press Ltd,
The Old Potato Station,
14 Howard Street South,
Belfast BT7 1AP
Tel: +44 (0) 28 90 243074
Fax: +44 (0) 28 90 246756
Web Site: www.appletree.ie
E-mail: reception@appletree.ie

The Appletree Book of Celtic Verse

A catalogue record for this book is available
from the British Library.

ISBN 0-86281-763-3

9 8 7 6 5 4 3 2 1

The Appletree Book

of

Celtic Verse

Compiled by W A Ross
Illustrated by Angela McCormick

INTRODUCTION

The poems in this collection come from Gaelic (Irish and Scots), Welsh, Cornish, Manx and Breton - from all the Celtic languages of the British Isles plus Brittany. Most of these have been translated into English more than once. It was with the Ossian poems of James Thomson, published between 1760 and 1763, that the English-speaking world became aware of the existence of an ancient poetic tradition reaching back into the past, long before the existence of English as a language. The spurious elements in Thomson's "translations" have long been public knowledge, but it was equally clear that there were genuine sources which the enterprising writer had improved on. Matthew Arnold for one, a poet with a keen interest in Celtic culture and no liking for shams, was prepared to award Thomson eternal credit for having opened the door on a new, remarkable and rewarding world of spirit and imagination.

Not the least part of Celtic poetry's appeal was the sense that it had retained vital links with its ancient roots. This was due primarily to the oral tradition - much of Celtic poetry had not been written down; or if it had, it had been largely lost. But for centuries, it was the practice and the pride of the Celtic bard both to preserve vast amounts of information in his mind - historical, genealogical, environmental - as well as verse; and of course to be able to extemporise at need in a whole variety of established poetic forms, producing celebrations, laments, arousals, reflections on events. One nineteenth-century writer called the Celtic tradition "a clear well" and there is no doubt that readers felt they were being brought in contact with an era where life was simpler, perhaps, but grander, and lived in harmony with the elements of a wild nature. It was a society in which heroes walked and were celebrated, where people felt near to, and at home with, the divine.

In the turbulent, changing world of the nineteenth-century, this was a wonderful formula for escape and association with a world far removed from steam, mass politics, and urban life, and yet whose physical substance, mountains, lakes and coasts, remained. This was the great era of tracking down Celtic verse and translating it. Inevitably the translations gave a colouring of their own time, and it was long before a critical scholarly reaction set in. In the twentieth-century, John Fraser, Oxford Professor of Celtic and a Gaelic speaker, could dismiss the work of one of the best-known popularisers of Celtic song, Kenneth Macleod, as "the bleatings of a sheep".

The subtlety of presentation in Celtic composition suits the preoccupations of a new generation, and today, elements of Celtic spirituality are being revealed which might have caused surprise or amusement to the bards of long ago. Every translation is an adventure and a discovery. However for the purist, there is no alternative to the timeless languages of the originals.

Celtic poetry in Welsh, Gaelic and Breton is still composed and the ancient languages, as the Scottish poet Somhairle MacGill-Eain observed, have had to come to terms not only with such things as the motor car, but with Freud and the atom bomb. This collection is not however concerned with contemporary writing; its time-span covers the centuries from the time before the Celts were Christians, up to the eighteenth-century, the period when the oral tradition and not the printed page was the context and the preserver of Celtic poetry.

AN INVOCATION

Bless, O Chief of generous Chiefs,
Myself and all that is near to me,
Bless me in all my actions,
Make me safe for ever,
Make me safe for ever.

From every brownie and banshee,
From very evil wish and sorrow,
From every sprite and water-wraith,
From every fairy-mouse and grass-mouse,
From every fairy-mouse and grass-mouse.

From every troll among the hills,
From every spirit hard-pressing me,
From every ghoul that haunts the glens,
O, save me till the end of my day,
O, save me till the end of my day.

CAOINE

Cold, dark and dumb lies my boy on his bed,
Cold, dark and silent the night dews are shed;
Hot, swift and fierce fall my tears for the dead!

His footprints lay light in the dew of the dawn,
As the straight, narrow track of the young mountain fawn;
But I'll ne'er again follow them over the lawn.

His manly cheek blushed with the sun's rising ray,
And he shone in his strength like the sun at mid-day;
But a black cloud of darkness has hid him away.

And that black cloud for ever shall cling to the skies;
And never, ah, never I'll see him arise,
Lost warmth of my bosom, lost light of my eyes!

CRINOG

(A Celtic monk's lament for his soul-sister)

Crinog of melodious song,
No longer young, but bashful-eyed,
As when we roved Niall's northern land,
Hand-in-hand or side by side.

Peerless maid, whose looks brimmed o'er
With the lovely lore of Heaven,
By whom I slept in dreamless joy,
A gentle boy of summers seven.

We dwelt in Banva's* broad domain,
Without one stain of soul or sense;
While still mine eye flashed forth on thee
Affection free of all offence.

* Ireland

13

THE MYSTERY OF AMERGIN

I am the wind which breathes upon the sea,

I am the ocean wave,

I am the murmur of the billows,

I am the ox of the seven combats,

I am the vulture of the rocks,

I am a sunbeam,

I am the fairest of plants,

I am a wild boar in valour,

I am a salmon in the water,

I am a lake in the plain,

I am a word of knowledge

I am the point of the lance of battle

I am the God who lights fire in the brain

Who is it who throws light into the meeting on the mountain?

Who announces the ages of the moon?

Who teaches the place where the sun makes his bed?

FAIRY SONG

O little Morag
A-climbing bens,
Descending glens,
A-climbing bens,
O little Morag
A-climbing bens,
Tired you are
- And the calves lost.

from THE WISH OF THE AGED BARD

Friends of my youth, farewell!
Farewell, ye maids of love!
I see you now no more - with you is summer still,
With me - the winter night.

O lay me by the roaring fall,
By the sound of the murmuring craig,
Let the harp and shell be near,
And the shield of my father's wars.

O breeze of Ocean come,
With the sound of thy gentle course,
Raise me on thy wings, O wind;
And bear me to the isle of rest;

Where the heroes of old are gone
To the sleep that wakes no more;
Open the hall of Ossian and Daol -
The night is come - the bard departs!

Behold my dim grey mist!
I go to the dwelling of bards on the hill!
Give me my airy harp and shell for the way -
And now - my own beloved harp and shell, farewell!

QUICK, DEATH

This room an ante-chamber is:
Beyond - the Hall of very Bliss!
Quick, Death! for underneath thy door,
I see the glimmering of Heaven's floor.

THE SWORD DANCE

Blood, wine and glee,
Sun, to you -
Blood, wine and glee!

Chorus
Fire, fire, steel, O steel!
Fire, fire! Steel and fire!
Oak! Oak, earth and waves!
Waves, oak, earth and oak!

Glee of dance and song,
And battle-throng -
Battle, dance and song!

Chorus

Let the sword-blades swing
In a ring -
Let the sword-blades swing!

Chorus

Song of the blue steel,
Death to feel -
Song of the blue steel!

Chorus

Fight, in which the sword
Is Lord -
Fight of the fell sword!

Chorus

Sword, you mighty king
Of battle's ring -
Sword, you mighty king!

Chorus

With the rainbow's light
Be you bright -
With the rainbow's light!

Fire, fire, steel, o steel!
Fire, fire! Steel and fire!
Oak! Oak, earth and waves!
Waves, oak, earth and oak!

from BEN DORAIN

I would rather have the deer
Gasping moaningly,
Than all Erin's songs to hear
Sung melodiously;
For above the finest bass
Has the stag's sweet voice a grace
As he bellows on the face
Of Ben Dorain.

from THE TERCETS OF LLYWARC'H

Entangling is the snare, clustered is the ash;
The ducks are in the pond; white breaks the wave;
More powerful than a hundred is the counsel of the heart.

Long the night, boisterous is the sea-shore;
Usual a tumult in a congregation;
The vicious will not agree with the good.

Long the night, boisterous is the mountain;
The wind whistles over the tops of trees;
Ill-nature will not deceive the discreet.

THE SONG OF FIONN

May-day, delightful time. How beautiful the colour.
The blackbirds sing their full tune. Would that Laeg were
here!
The cuckoos call in constant strains. How welcome is the
noble
Brilliance of the changing season. On the margin of the
branchy woods,
The summer swallows skim the stream; swift horses seek
the pool:
The heather spreads her long hair out; pale bog-myrtle
thrives;
The sea is lulled to calm, flowers cover the earth.

HOSPITALITY

1
Whether my house is dark or bright,
I close it not on any wight,
Lest Thou, the King of Stars so great,
Should shut me out from Heaven's gate.

2
If from a guest who shares thy board,
Thy dearest dainty thou shalt hoard,
Not just thy guest, O never doubt it,
But Mary's Son shall go without it.

Mannin Veen

Stranger, if thou seekest ease,
Safety, quiet and sweet peace,
If of rest thou would'st be sure,
Lovest sober joys and pure.
To the hills and valleys green,
Come then, come to Mannin Veen

Traveller, seek no foreign strand,
Thou wilt find no lovelier land;
Take the word of one who knows
How our life here smoothly flows.
Stranger, leave not this fair scene,
Make thy home in Mannin Veen.

With its hills and valleys green,
Come then, come,
Come, oh! come,
Come, oh! come to Mannin Veen.

THE RUNE OF ST PATRICK

(The Cry of the Deer)

At Tara today in this fateful hour
I place all Heaven with its power,
And the sun with its brightness,
And the snow with its whiteness,
And fire with all the strength it hath,
And lightning with its sudden wrath,
And the winds with their speed along their path,
And the sea with its deeps.
And the rocks with their steeps,
And the earth with its starkness:
All these I place,
By God's almighty help and grace,
Between myself and the powers of darkness.

THE SCRIBE

For weariness my hand writes ill,
My small sharp quill runs rough and slow;
Its slender beak with failing craft
Gives forth its draught of dark-blue flow.

And yet God's blessed wisdom gleams
And streams beneath my fair brown palm,
As the quick jets of holly ink
The letters link of prayer or psalm.

So still my dripping pen I take
And make my mark on parchment white,
Unceasing, at some rich man's call,
Till wearied all am I tonight.

St Columba On Iona

Delightful would it be to me
From a rock pinnacle to trace
Continually
The Ocean's face:
That I might watch the heaving waves
Of noble force
To God the Father chant their staves
Of the earth's course.
That I might mark its level strand,
To me no lone distress,
That I might mark the sea-birds' wondrous band -
Sweet source of happiness.
That I might hear the sounding billows thunder
On the rough beach.
That by my holy church side I might ponder
Their mighty speech;
Or watch surf-skimming gulls the dark shoal follow
With joyful scream,
Or giant ocean monsters spout and wallow,
Wonder supreme!
That I might well observe of ebb and flood
All cycles therein;
And that my mystic name might be for good
But *Cul-ri Erin.**

That gazing toward her on my heart might fall
A full contrition,

That I might then bewail my evils all,
Though hard the admission;
That I might bless the Lord who all things orders
For their great good.
The countless hierarchies through Heaven's bright
borders -
Land, strand and flood.
That I might search all books and in their chart
Find my soul's calm;
Now kneel before the Heaven of my heart,
Now chant a psalm;
Now meditate upon the King of Heaven,
Chief of the Holy Three;
Now ply my work by no compulsion driven,
What greater joy could be?
Now picking dulse upon the rocky shore,
Now fishing eager on,
Now furnishing food unto the starving poor
In hermitage anon.
The guidance of the King of Kings
Has been vouchsafed unto me;
If I keep watch beneath His wings
No evil shall undo me.

* Literally, "back turned to Ireland"

MERLIN THE DIVINER

Merlin, Merlin! where are you going,
So early in the day, with your black dog?

I have come here to search the way,
To find the red egg;
The red egg of the sea serpent,
By the sea-side in the hollow of the stone.
I am going to seek in the valley
The green water-cress, and the golden grass,
And the topmost branch of oak,
In the wood by the side of the fountain.

Merlin, Merlin! retrace your steps;
Leave the branch on the oak,
And the green water-cress in the valley,
As well as the golden grass;
And leave the sea serpent's red egg,
In the foam by the hollow of the stone.
Merlin, Merlin! retrace your steps -
There is no diviner but God.

The Enchanted Valley

I will go where lilies blow
And linger by the languid streams,
Within that vale where jewels glow;
Where bright-winged dreams flit to and fro,
I long its magic peace to know.

Beware! Beware that vale so fair!
A hollow phantom you will be -
Bereft alike of joy and care,
You hunger for life's burden there
And ever cry, "Beware, beware!"

LOVE OF MY HEART

Oh graih my chree, will you not follow me?
Oh love of my heart, oh awake, awake!
If I'll not get your love, and you to stay with me,
Then I must give Death my heart to break.

Oh, love has filled my heart with sorrow
And filled my mind with a heavy grief;
Now sleep has left my house, and rest returns not,
I seek them vainly, and find no relief.

WHAT IS LOVE?

A love much-enduring through a year is my love,
It is grief in the heart,
It is stretching of strength beyond its bounds,
It is the four quarters of the world,
It is the highest height of heaven,
It is breaking of the neck,
It is battle with a spectre,
It is drowning with water,
It is a race against heaven,
It is champion-deeds beneath the sea,
It is wooing the echo;
So is my love, and my passion,
And my devotion to her to whom I gave them.

Deirdre's Farewell To Alba

Glen Etive! O, Glen Etive!
There I raised my earliest house;
Beautiful its woods on rising
Where the sun fell on Glen Etive.

Glen Orchy! O, Glen Orchy!
The straight glen of smooth ridges;
No man of the age was so joyful
As Naois in Glen Orchy.

Glenlaidhe! O, Glenlaidhe!
I used to sleep by its soothing murmurs;
Fish, and flesh of wild boar and badger
Was my repast in Glenlaidhe.

Glendaruadh! O, Glendaruadh!
I love each man of its inheritance;
Sweet the noise of the cuckoo on bending bow,
On the hill above Glendaruadh.
Glenmasan! O, Glenmasan!
High its herbs, fair its boughs;
Solitary was the place of our repose,
On grassy Invermasan.

THE WORST WAY OF PLEADING

'O Cormac MacArt, of wisdom exceeding,
What is the evilest way of pleading?'
Said Cormac, 'Not hard to tell.
Against knowledge contending,
Without proofs, pretending;
In bad language escaping;
A style stiff and scraping;
Speech mean and muttering;
Hair-splitting, stuttering;
Uncertain proofs devising;
Authorities despising;
Scorning custom's reading;
Confusing all your pleading;
To madness a mob be leading;
With the shout of a strumpet,
Blowing one's own trumpet!'

THE HARP

The harp to everyone is dear
Who hateth vice and all things evil;
Hail to its gentle voice so clear,
Its gentle voice affrights the Devil.

The Devil cannot the Minstrel quell:
He by the Minstrel is confounded;
From Saul was cast the spirit fell,
When David's harp melodious sounded.

A HIGHLAND LULLABY

I left my baby lying here, lying here, lying here -
I left my baby lying here,
To go and gather blaeberries.

Hó-bhan, hó-bhan, Goiridh òg O,
Goiridh òg O, Goiridh òg O,
Hó-bhan, hó-bhan, Goiridh òg-O,
I've lost my darling baby, O

I found the small brown otter's track,
The otter's track, the otter's track -
I found the small brown otter's track,
But never found my baby, O

Hó-bhan, hó-bhan, etc.

I found the track of the swan on the loch,
The swan on the loch, the swan on the loch -
I found the track of the swan on the loch,
But never found my baby, O.

Hó-bhan, hó-bhan, etc.

I found the track of the yellow fawn,
The yellow fawn, the yellow fawn -
I found the track of the yellow fawn,
But never found my baby, O.

Hó-bhan, hó-bhan, etc.

I found the trail of the mountain mist,
The mountain mist, the mountain mist -
I found the trail of the mountain mist,
But never found my baby, O

Hó-bhan, hó-bhan, etc.

ADVICE TO A PILGRIM

Unto Rome thou woulds't attain?
Great the toil is, small the gain,
If the King thou seek'st therein,
Travel not with thee from Erin.

The Church Bell In The Night

Sweet little bell, sweet little bell,
Struck long and well upon the wind,
I'd rather tryst with thee tonight
Than any maiden light of mind.

Invocation

Read these faint runes of Mystery,
O Celt, at home and o'er the sea;
The bond is loosed - the poor are free -
The world's great future rests with thee.

Till the soil - bid cities rise -
Be strong, O Celt, be rich, be wise -
But still, with those divine grave eyes,
Respect the Realm of Mysteries.

from *The Book of Orm*

from SONG TO THE WIND

Discover you what is
The strong creature from before the Flood,
Without flesh, without bone,
Without vein, without blood,
Without head, without feet;
It will be neither older nor younger
Than at the beginning;
For fear of a denial,
These are no rude wants
With creatures.
Great God! how the sea whitens
When first it comes!
Great are its gusts
When it comes from the south;
How it dries the air
When it strikes upon coasts.
It is in the field, in the wood,
Without hand and without foot,
Without signs of age,
Though it be as old as
The five ages or periods;
And older still,
Though they be numberless years.
It is also so wide
As the surface of the earth;
And it was not born, nor ever seen.
It will cause consternation
Wherever God willeth,

On sea and on land,
It neither sees, nor is seen.
Its course is devious,
And it will not come when desired -
On sea and on land
We cannot do without it.

OMENS

I heard the cuckoo, with no food in my stomach,
I heard the stock-dove on the top of the tree,
I heard the sweet singer in the farther copse,
I heard the screech of the night-owls.

I saw the lamb, with his back to me,
I saw the snail on his bare flag-stone,
I saw the foal, with his rump to me,
I saw the wheatear on a dike of holes,
I saw the snipe while sitting bent.

And I foresaw that the year
Would not go well with me.

THE FAIRY-KING'S CALL

O Befind, wilt thou come with me
To the wondrous land of melody?
The crown of their head like the primrose fair,
Their bodies below as the colour of snow.

There in that land is no *mine* or *thine*;
White the teeth there, eyebrows black,
Brilliant the eyes - great is the host -
And each cheek the hue of the foxglove.

How heady so ever the ale of Inis Fàl,
More intoxicating the ale of the Great Land;
A marvel among lands, the land of which I speak;
No young man there enters upon old age.

Like the purple of the plain each neck,
Like the ousel's egg the colour of the eye;
Though fair to the sight are the plains of Fàl,
They are a desert to him who knows the Great Plains.

We behold every one on every side,
And none beholds us;
The gloom of Adam's sin it is
Conceals us from their reckoning.

O woman, if thou wilt come among my strong people,
A golden crown shall grace thy head;
Fresh swine-flesh, new milk and ale for drink
Thou shalt have with me, O woman fair!

OSSIAN'S LAMENT

Long was last night in cold Elphin,
More long is tonight on its weary way.
Though yesterday seemed to me long and ill,
Yet longer still was this dreary day.

And long for me is each hour new-born,
Stricken, sad and smitten with grief
For the hunting lands and the Fenian bands,
And the long-haired, generous Fenian chief.

I hear no music, I find no feast,
I slay no beast from my prancing steed,
I bestow no gold, I am poor and old,
I am sick and cold, without wine or mead.

I court no more, and I hunt no more,
These were before my great delight.
I cannot slay, and I take no prey;
Weary the day and long the night.
No heroes come in battle array,
No game I play; there is nought to win.
I swim no stream with my men of might;
Long is the night in cold Elphin.

Ask, O Patrick, thy God of grace,
To tell me the place he will place me in,
And save my soul from the Ill One's might,
For long is tonight in cold Elphin.

The lions of the hill are gone,
And I am left alone - alone -
Dig the grave both wide and deep,
For I am sick, and fain would sleep!

The falcons of this wood are flown,
And I am left alone - alone -
Dig the grave both deep and wide,
And let us slumber side by side.

The dragons of the rock are sleeping,
Sleep that wakes not for our weeping -
Dig the grave, and make it ready,
Lay me on my true love's body.
...
Lay upon the low grave floor,
'Neath each head, the sword he bore;
Many a time the warlike three
Reddened their blue blades for me.

Lay the collars, as is meet,
Of the greyhounds at their feet;
Many a time for me have they
Brought the great red deer to bay.

...

Woe to Emain, roof and wall!
Woe to Red Branch, hearth and hall!
Tenfold woe and black dishonour
To the foul and false Clan Conor.

Dig the grave both wide and deep,
Sick I am, and fain would sleep.
Dig the grave and make it ready,
Lay me on my true love's body.

THE YARROW

I will pluck the yarrow fair,
That kindlier shall be my face,
That more warm shall be my lips,
That more chaste shall be my speech,
Be my speech the beams of the sun,
Be my lips the sap of the strawberry.

May I be an isle in the sea,
May I be a hill on the shore,
May I be a star in the dark time,
May I be a staff to the weak:
Wound can I every man,
Wound can no man me.

I Am Watching My Young Calves Sucking

I am watching my young calves sucking:
Who are you that would put me out of of my luck?
Can I not be walking, can I not be walking,
Can I not be walking on my own farm-lands?

I will not for ever go back before you;
If I must needs be submissive to you, great is my grief;
If I cannot be walking, if I cannot be walking,
If I cannot be walking on my own farm-lands.

Little heed I pay, and 'tis little my desire,
Your fine blue cloak and your bright birds' plumes,
If I cannot be walking, if I cannot be walking,
If I cannot be walking on my own farm-lands!
There is a day coming, it is plain to my eyes,
When there will not be among us the mean likes of you;
But each will be walking, each will be walking,
Wherever he will, on his own farm-land.

OSSIAN SANG

Sweet is the voice in the land of gold,
And sweeter the music of birds that soar,
When the cry of the heron is heard on the wold,
And the waves break softly on Bundatrore.

Down floats on the murmuring of the breeze
The call of the cuckoo from Cossahun,
The blackbird is warbling among the trees,
And soft is the kiss of the warming sun.

The cry of the eagle of Assaroe
O'er the court of MacMorne to me is sweet,
And sweet is the cry of the bird below
Where the wave and the wind and the tall cliff meet.

Finn MacCool is the father of me,
Whom seven battalions of Fenians fear:
When he launches his hounds on the open lea,
Grand is their cry as they rouse the deer.

MOLING SANG THIS

When I with the old consort
Jest and sport they straight lay by;
When with frolic youth I'm flung,
Maddest of the young am I.

THE MONK AND HIS WHITE CAT

Pangar, my white cat, and I
Silent ply our special crafts;
Hunting mice his one pursuit,
Mine to shoot keen spirit shafts.

For me no pleasure can exceed
Reading, absorbed in some rare book;
Yet white Pangar, at his play
Offers me no jealous look.

Thus together in one cell
Our time is spent - and far from dull;
Each one at his private task,
Finds that his life is rich and full.

See Pangar pounce upon his mouse,
With claws and jaws contrive the kill;
While I a meaning subtly framed
Hold in mind with studious thrill.

Now his green and lambent gaze
Surveys in hope the hollow wall;
My dimmer vision also seeks
To pierce the dark and see the whole.

Pangar springs with fearsome joy
To seize his prey in talons keen;
Problems difficult and dear
I stalk, and wisdom hope to glean.

Crossing not each other's will,
Diverse still, yet still allied,
Following each his own lone ends,
Constant friends we here abide.

Pangar, master of his art,
Plays his part in supple youth,
While I sedately strive to clear
Shadows from the light of Truth.

from THE SONG OF THE THRUSH

From the branches of the hazel
Of broad green leaves
He sings an ode
To God the Creator;
With a carol of love
From the green glade,
To all in the hollow
Of the glen, who love him;
Balm of the heart
To those who love.
I had from his beak
The voice of inspiration,
A metric song
That gratified me;
Glad was I made
By his minstrelsy.
Then respectfully
Uttered I an address
From the stream of the vale
To the bird.
My urgent request,
His undertaking a message
To the fair one
In whom dwells my affection.
Gone is the bard of the leaves
From the small twigs
To the second Lunet,
The sun of maidens!

To the streams of the plain,
St Mary prosper him,
To bring to me,
Under the green woods
The colour of one night's snow
Without delay.

THE MARCH OF THE FAERIE HOST

In well-planned battle array,
Ahead of their fair chieftain,
They march wielding blue spears,
White, curly-headed bands.

They scatter the armies of the foe,
They ravage every land,
Splendidly they march to battle
Impetuous, glamorous, avenging host!

No wonder that their strength be great:
Sons of kings and queens are one and all.
On all their heads are set
Beautiful manes of yellow-gold.

Their bodies comely, smooth,
Their eyes bright, blue-starred,
Pure crystal their teeth,
Thin their red lips:

Good they are at man-slaying.

EPITAPH ON THE BARD IAIN LOM

Mightier was the verse of Iain,
Hearts to nerve, to kindle eyes,
Than the claymore of the valiant,
Than the counsel of the wise.

COLIN'S CATTLE

A maiden sang sweetly
As a bird on a tree,
Cro' Chailean, Cro' Chailean,
Cro' Chailean for me!

My own Colin's cattle,
Dappled, dun, brown and grey,
They return to the milking
At the close of the day.

In the morning they wander
To the pastures afar,
Where the grass grows the greenest,
By corrie and scaur.

But so far as they wander,
Dappled, dun, brown and grey,
They return to the milking
At the close of the day.

My bed's in the Shian
On the cannach's soft down,
But I'd sleep best with Colin
In our shieling alone.

Thus a maiden sang sweetly
As a bird on a tree,
Cro' Chailean, Chro' Chailean,
Cro' Chailean for me.

from A SONG OF EXILE

I sit on a knoll,
All sorrowful and sad,
And I look on the grey sea
In mistiness clad,
And I brood on strange chances
That drifted me here,
Where Scarba and Jura
And Islay lie near.

Where Scarba and Jura
And Islay are near;
Grand land of rough mountains,
I wish thee good cheer.
I wish young Sir Norman
On mainland and islands
To be named with proud honour
First chief in the Highlands!

To be praised with proud honour,
First chief in the Highlands,
For wisdom and valour
In far and in nigh lands;
For mettle and manhood,
There's none may compare,
With the handsome Macleod
Of the princeliest air.

And the blood in his veins
Proclaims him the heir
Of the kings of Lochlann;
It flows rich and rare.
Each proud earl in Alba
Is knit with his line,
And Erin shakes hands with him
Over the brine.

And Erin shakes hands with him
Over the brine;
Brave son of brave father,
The pride of his line.
In camp and in council
Whose virtue was seen,
Whose purse was as free
As his claymore was keen.

THE HERMIT TO THE KING

I have a shieling in the wood,
None save my God has knowledge of it,
An ash-tree and a hazelnut
Its two sides shut; great oak boughs roof it.

Two heath-clad posts beneath a buckle
Of honeysuckle its frame are propping,
The woods around its narrow bound
Swine-feeding mast are richly dropping.

From out my shieling not too small,
Familar all, fair paths invite me;
And, blackbird, from my gable end,
Sweet sable friend, your notes delight me.

What though in kingly pleasures now
Beyond all riches you rejoice,
Content am I my Saviour good
Should on this wood have set my choice.

SONG OF THE RIVER-SPRITE NIGHEAG

I am washing the shrouds of the fair men
Who are going out but never shall come in;
The death-dirge of the ready-handed men
Who shall go out, seek peril and fall.

I am lustring the linen of the fair men
Who shall go out in the morning early,
Upon the well-shod grey steeds
And shall not return in season due.

THE OUTLAW'S SONG

"Who is that without
With voice like a sword,
That batters my bolted door?"

"I am Eamonn an Chnuic,
Cold, weary and wet
From long walking mountains and glens."

"O dear and bright love,
What would I do for you
But cover you with a skirt of my dress.
For shots full thick
Are raining on you,
And together we may be slaughtered!"

"Long am I out
Under snows, under frost,
Without comradeship with any,
My team unyoked,
My fallow unsown,
And they lost to me entirely;
Friend I have none
- I am heavy for that -
That would shelter me later or early,
And so I must go
East over the sea,
Since 'tis there I have no kindred."

To The Fox That Killed His Peacock

The wretch my starry bird who slew,
Beast of the flameless ember hue,
Assassin, glutton of the night,
Mixed of all creatures that are vile,
Land lobster, fugitive from light,
You coward mountain crocodile;
With downcast eye and ragged tail
Lurking in the hollow rocks,
Thief, ever ready to assail
The undefended flocks.
Your brassy breast and shaggy locks
Shall not protect you from the hound,
When with piercing eye he mocks
Your mazy refuge underground;
Whilst o'er my peacock's broken plumes shall shine
A pretty bower of faery eglantine.

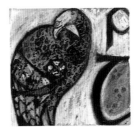

MONALTRI

There's a cry on the hill,
Not of joy but of ailing;
Dark-hair'd women mourn -
Beat their hands, with loud wailing.

They cry out, Ochon!
For the young Monaltri,
Who went to the hill,
But home came not he.

Without snood, without plaid,
Catriona's gone roaming;
O Catriona, my dear!
Homeward be
coming.

Och, hear, on the castle,
Yon pretty bird singing,
'Snoodless and plaidless,
Her hands she is wringing.'

THE CALENDS OF WINTER

The Calends of Winter are come; the grain
Grows hard; the dead leaf drops in the rain;
Though the stranger bid thee, turn not again.

The Calends of Winter: about the hearth
Draw the gossips close, as storm holds the earth;
Now many a secret spills in the mirth.

The Calends of Winter: forgot in the cold
The tale the Calends of Summer told -
What the cuckoo sang to the blackbird bold.

The Calends of Winter: the night falls soon,
Black as the raven; the afternoon
Declines to evening without a tune.

The Calends of Winter are come. The heath
Is bare where it was burnt. The breath
Of the oxen smokes. The old await death.

from THE LAMENT FOR GREGOR MacGREGOR

On an oaken block they laid him,
And they spilt his blood around,
I'd have drunk it in a glassful
Before it reached the ground

...

While the rest have all got lovers,
Now a lover have I none:
My fair blossom, fresh and fragrant,
Withers on the ground alone

...

Greatly better be with Gregor
In a mantle rude and torn,
Than with little Lowland barons
Where fine silks and lace are worn.

Bahu, bahu, little nursling,
Oh, so tender now and weak!
I fear the day will never brighten
When revenge for him you'll seek.

SHE

The white bloom of the blackthorn, she,
The small, sweet raspberry-blossom, she;
More fair the shy, rare glance of her eye
Than the world's wealth to me.

My heart's pulse, my secret, she,
The flower of the fragrant apple, she;
A summer glow over winter snow,
'Twixt Christmas and Easter, she.

AT THE WAVE-MOUTH

And who may the strange one be,
Who croons beside the wave-mouth,
Like sea-wrack brown and beauteous,
Who may yon strange one be?

Nor merle she nor mavis she,
St Bride's bird she nor sea-mew,
Nor seal from faraway linns,
Nor kyle sea-maiden she.

And who may the strange one be,
Who croons beside the wave-mouth,
Like sea-wrack brown and beauteous,
Who may yon strange one be?

THE DREAM OF THE KING OF BRITAIN

(A waulking song)

Britain's sleeping king beheld,
The loveliest maid beneath the sun;
He'd rather win her regard
Than converse with others like himself.

Said *Fios-fallaich** with good-will,
I myself will go and search for her;
I and my ghillie and my dog,
Let us set out this maid to find.

'Tis I myself own a ship,
Very swift to leave a wave behind;
I also have a good dog,
Most quick to set his eye to the chase.

*Veiled knowledge

THE HILL-WATER

Where dark water-cresses grow
You will trace its quiet flow,
With mossy border yellow,
So mild, so soft, and mellow,
In its pouring.
With no slimy dregs to trouble
The brightness of its bubble
As it threads its silver way
From the granite shoulders grey
Of Ben Dorain

Through rich green solitudes,
And steeply hanging woods
With blossom and with bell,
In rich redounding swell,
And the pride
Of the mountain daisy there,
And the forest everywhere,
With the dress and with the air
Of a bride.

THE STREAMS OF NANTSIAN

O the streams of Nantsian in two parts divide,
Where the young men in dancing meet sweetheart and
bride,
They will take no denial, we must frolic and sing,
And the sound of the viol, o it makes my heart ring.

On the rocky cliff yonder a castle upstands;
To the seamen a wonder, above the black sands.
'Tis of ivory builded, with diamonds glazed bright,
And with gold it is gilded, to shine in the night.

Over yonder high mountain the wild fowl do fly;
And in ocean's deep sounding the fairest pearls lie.
On eagle's wings soaring, I'll speed as the wind;
Ocean's fountain exploring, my true love I'll find.

O the streams of Nantsian divide in two parts,
And rejoin as in dancing do lads their sweethearts.
So the streams, bright and shining, though parted in
twain,
Reunite, intertwining, one thenceforth remain.

THE LAMENT FOR MacCRIMMON

Round Coolin's peak the mist is sailing,
The banshee croons her note of wailing,
Mild blue eyes with sorrow are streaming,
For him that shall no more return, MacCrimmon!

The breeze of the brae is mournfully blowing,
The brook on the hillside is plaintively flowing,
The warblers, the soul of the groves, are moaning,
For MacCrimmon that's gone, with no hope of returning.

The tearful clouds the stars are veiling,
The sails are spread, but the boat is not sailing,
The waves of the sea are moaning and mourning
For MacCrimmon that's gone to find no more returning.

No more on the hill at the festal meeting
The pipe shall sound with echo repeating,
And lads and lasses change from mirth to mourning
For him that is gone to know no more returning.

No more, no more, no more for ever,
In war or peace, shall return MacCrimmon;
No more, no more, no more for ever,
Shall love or gold bring back MacCrimmon!

A MANX LULLABY

When lilacs are lush and bees in the blossom,
When cuckoos are calling and blackbirds do sing;
O sleep in your silence, babe of my bosom,
As through the green boughs your cradle I swing.

Oh hush you, my baby,
O hush you, my love.

O smile in your sleeping, my beautiful baby,
Although our ship's rocking, and waves they rise high;
Far o'er the wild water, wherever our way be,
O child of my heart, 'tis safe you shall lie.

O hush you, my baby,
O hush you, my love.

On green hills afar the shadows they darken,
The moon's silver cradle is shining above;
Within it I'll lay you, and there you shall hearken
The songs that the stars sing, O child of my love.

O hush you, my baby,
O hush you, my love.

INDEX